FAMILIAR SUBJECTS

The photographs in this book are actual
size reproductions of Polaroid SX-70 prints made
with a Polaroid SX-70 Alpha 1 camera. The
prints have been hand worked as described in the
essay beginning on page eighty-five.

FAMILIAR SUBJECTS

POLAROID SX-70 IMPRESSIONS BY

NORMAN LOCKS

A Headlands Press Book

PUBLISHED IN SAN FRANCISCO BY

HARPER & ROW, PUBLISHERS

NEW YORK · HAGERSTOWN · SAN FRANCISCO · LONDON

To Suzy, Anna, and James

Produced by The Headlands Press, Inc.
San Francisco, California

Library of Congress Catalog Number 78-4754
ISBN 0-06-250530-0 (paper)
ISBN 0-06-250531-9 (cloth)

Color separations for prints number 2, 6, 14,
15, 34, 35, 42, 43, 68, and 75 provided courtesy of
Friends of Photography, Carmel, California

'Polaroid' and 'SX-70' are registered trademarks
of Polaroid Corporation,
Cambridge, Massachusetts, U.S.A.

Acknowledgements

The photographs in this book would not have been made without the support and love of Rogier Gregoire. Greg put the SX-70 in my hands and helped keep it loaded during my first years with the camera.

As a workshop director I have had the opportunity to work with some of the finest photographers in the world. I am grateful to each instructor who shared in those workshops, especially Robert Heinecken, Ansel Adams, Dave Bohn, and Ralph Gibson.

This project would not have begun if Lynn Miller, a friend for many years and editor of *Small Farmer's Journal* in Junction City, Oregon, had not introduced Andrew Fluegelman to my photographs. Nor could it have been completed without Andrew's enthusiasm for both the photographs and the spirit in which they were done.

My thanks to Barry Traub, Andrew Fluegelman, Molly Prescott, and Howard Jacobsen of The Headlands Press, which produced this book, and the people at Harper & Row, San Francisco, whose excitement and confidence made its publication possible.

I wish to acknowledge most of all my parents, Seymour and Fay Locks, who have encouraged all my efforts and loved me through my struggles.

Foreword

I was introduced to Norman Locks' photographs when Lynn Miller happened to show me the catalog from Norman's exhibit at the Friends of Photography. The catalog contained color reproductions of ten of his works: pictures of bottles on a refrigerator, an old typewriter, some legs propped in front of a portable TV, tea being poured, the back of a woman in blue light. These familiar subjects each seemed to hold a mystery.

I looked at the pictures very closely, until my eyes were only a couple of inches from the page, and still I could not unravel the detail or assign limits to the depth of the colors. Snatches of photo-realism collided with finely etched tracings and gentle brush strokes. These pictures were beautiful, and challenging. I could not comprehend how they had been produced. "Are these really photographs?" I asked. When I was told that they were taken with a Polaroid SX-70 camera and then hand worked with a dental tool, I immediately phoned Norman Locks and made a date to see for myself.

Norman was teaching at the University of California at Santa Cruz and was living with his family at the La Bahia Apartments along the Santa Cruz boardwalk and beach. His living room was dominated by a large table on which dozens of SX-70 film boxes had been recycled into files containing prints in varying stages of completion. Beyond that, his 'studio' or 'dark-room' consisted of a masonite drawing board and a box of stylus-like objects. Norman's art required minimal equipment and space.

We went out for lunch, Norman carrying with him his folded Alpha 1 camera. As we introduced our-selves over soup, salad, and tea, Norman stuck a flashbar on his camera, focused on the edge of the table, and pressed the shutter. In a second and a half, his SX-70 ejected a print. A few minutes later the blue-green surface cleared to reveal an ordered composition of bean sprouts, sugar bowl, and flower vase. Norman had casually invested our table setting with the same immediacy and romance of the images I had seen in the catalog. There was no pretentious-ness in the act. Picture-taking with the SX-70 was ir-resistible fun, and Norman displayed obvious delight at the Tom Swift wizardry that each push of the but-ton promised.

We spent the rest of the day looking at Norman's finished pieces, and I began to realize the extent to which the subject matter of his pictures chronicled his family's daily lives. After having just looked at the prints reproduced in this book as numbers 13 and 70, we walked to the beach with Norman's son James and tossed that same rubber football, returning to be greeted by his daughter Anna and her teddy bear 'Rocky'. Anna's mother, Suzy, was wearing the same plaid shirt and jeans as in the print that is now on the cover of this book. I was invited to stay for dinner, in company with the very kitchen utensils, flower set-tings, and random objects that populate Norman's work. Norman's photographs are not contrived. His subjects come from across the room or, at most, across the street. In this sense, he has remained faithful to the spirit of the SX-70 as the perfect snap-shot camera for birthday parties, ball games, and barbecues.

What had really brought me to Santa Cruz was the chance to witness the technique that created out of snapshots echoes of Degas and Monet. Norman agreed to a demonstration and produced a pencil-sized instrument similar to the one a dentist uses for routine check-ups. He began to make impressions on the picture taken that afternoon in the cafe. He worked quickly and freely, outlining the predominant forms and reducing irrelevant aspects of the print to milky gray crosshatching. The process was much like drawing, except the emulsion of the print itself was being altered while still within its protective plastic sandwich.

As Norman worked, the subjects of the photograph achieved a new presence. The print was no longer a frozen momento delivered automatically by the camera. It was a vision transformed, tempered by all the synapses between eye and hand. As much as the taking of the photograph had been Norman's creation, the print was now indisputably his own.

It was an infectious experience. By the next afternoon, I had gained access to an SX-70 camera, bought a couple of boxes of film, and collected an assortment of pointed tools for drawing.

I hope that all readers of this book will try their hands at making their own SX-70 impressions, as I did, because I believe they will discover two things. First, they are likely to enjoy a new sense of connectedness and power in the prints they make, regardless of whether they are professional photographers, serious hobbyists, or occasional snapshooters. Nothing can compare to seeing a developed print minutes after the event and then restructuring it by one's own hand work. It is a joyfully unnerving process.

Second, I am confident that anyone who tries making their own SX-70 impressions will appreciate what exceptional results Norman Locks has achieved with this new art form. Because the process itself is simple, it requires sensitivity, diligence, and talent to turn snapshots into provocative images.

In the course of producing this book, I have developed a great admiration and respect for Norman Locks. It is rare to find someone so personally committed to his art and so willing to share it. I have looked at his photographs many, many times and am still making discoveries in them. I hope that everyone will delight in making many of their own.

ANDREW FLUEGELMAN
Editor, The Headlands Press

FAMILIAR SUBJECTS

3

4

9

10

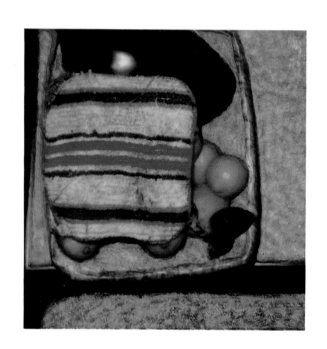

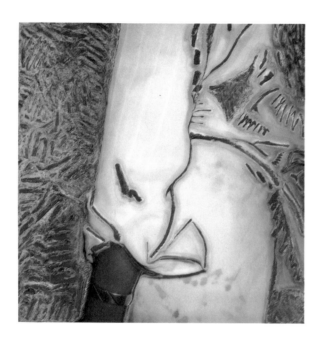

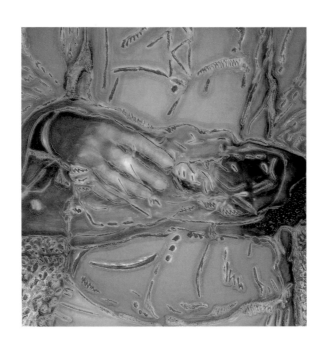

25

27

28

31   32

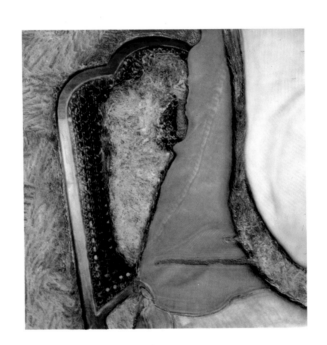

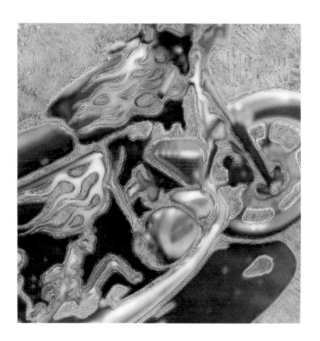

38
39

42

43

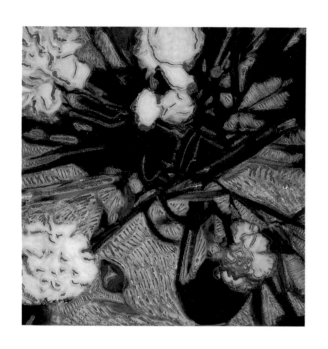

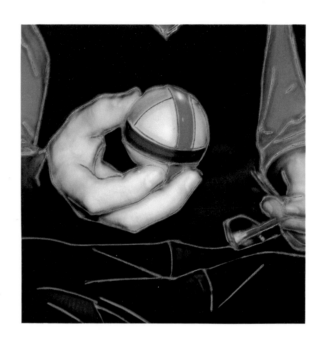

48

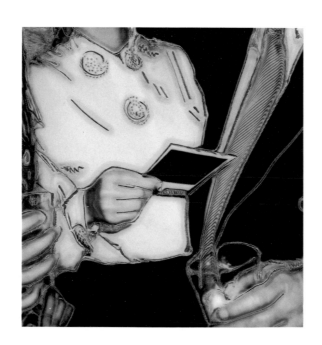

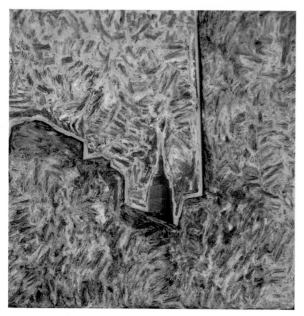

55

56

58

59

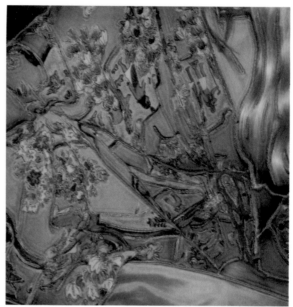

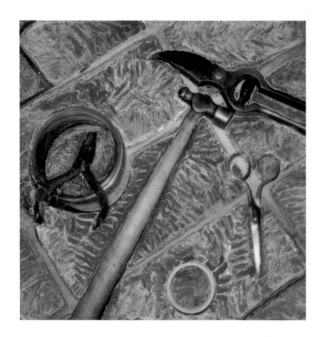

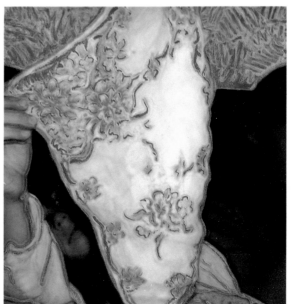

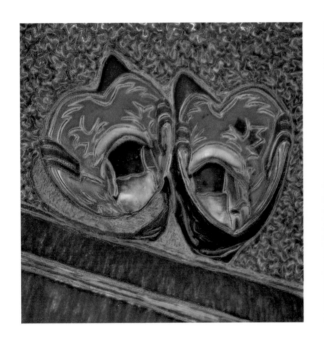

72

73

74

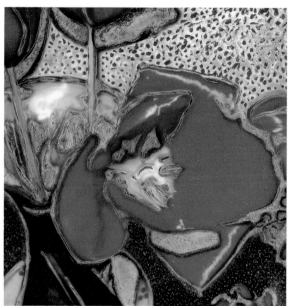

83

Catalog

SX-70 Impressions: Techniques and Possibilities

The work in this book grew out of playfulness and an addiction to the magic of the SX-70 camera. From the very first photograph I took using the camera, I was intrigued by the picture-making process. As I watched the development of the SX-70 print in my hands, I recalled the mystification I felt at the age of thirteen when I printed my first black and white images. I had no idea, however, that the SX-70 would become such a dominant tool in my growth as a photographer.

During the first year I used the SX-70 camera, my photographs were not distinguishable from anyone else's family pictures: shots of my children in and about the house, of friends and gatherings, of places visited, and of subjects that simply appealed to me. I used the SX-70 as a snapshot camera. Then, in the summer of 1976, I was conducting a series of photography workshops and my family and I were living in a VW camper. Throughout the summer, I made dozens of photographs—experimenting, playing, and learning daily.

I began drawing on my SX-70 prints out of curiosity. Having seen manipulated SX-70 work of other photographers, I was aware that the emulsion remained soft for a few days and could be altered. Although my first attempts at drawing on my

ANDREW FLUEGELMAN

THE PHOTOGRAPHER 'DRAWING' ON A PRINT

input and control was compensated for by the addition of the drawing technique. It satisfied both my interest in the photographic process, with its characteristic tie to reality, and my appreciation for the highly personal nature of hand work.

Although I frequently refer to a 'drawing technique', the images in this book were created by applying only pressure to the mylar on the front of the SX-70 print after it is ejected from the camera. The physical act is much like drawing with a pencil or a pen, but nothing is deposited on the surface of the picture. Instead, the pressure breaks down and mixes the emulsion layers which are sandwiched in the print between the top layer of mylar and the black backing. Depending on the tool used, the amount of pressure applied, and the nature of the emulsion itself, new lines, forms, and textures can be created.

pictures did not produce exceptional images, the process itself was immediately exciting to me. It indicated a way by which the structure and form of the original image could be unified.

The SX-70 is essentially an automatic camera. The camera chooses a combination of shutter speed and aperture and then delivers a developed picture without personal assistance. For me, this limitation of

This process can be practiced on any picture taken with Polaroid SX-70 film. I used a Polaroid SX-70 Alpha I camera to photograph all the images in this book, but as the entire drawing process takes place after the print is ejected from the camera, it is not dependent on the particular model camera used. The 'peel-apart' Polaroid instant films, and the Kodak instant films, have a different emulsion structure and cannot be manipulated in the same manner.

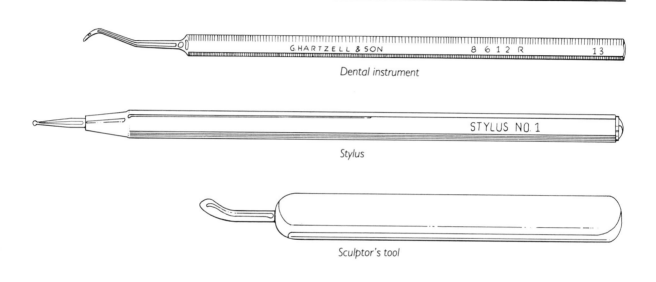

Dental instrument

Stylus

Sculptor's tool

TOOLS FOR HAND WORKING

Virtually any firm object can be used to draw on the print, and each tool creates its own effect. Both pointed and blunt objects work well. For most of my hand work, I use a dental instrument which has a curved end that comes to a point. The design of this tool gives me a great deal of control. The particular shape of the point makes it possible to produce both fine and broad lines, and the curved end is ideal for working large areas. I use a ball-point stylus and a leather punch to produce various dotted effects.

I am continually experimenting with new tools. My father is a sculptor, and I have adapted some implements from his studio. One day I found a piece of bone on the beach which could push broad areas of emulsion to the edges of the print. The dental tool serves this same purpose, but I enjoy using the bone.

Following is a list of objects that one might use for a particular effect. I have not tried them all:

- pencils
- pens
- coins
- keys
- knives
- forks
- spoons
- chopsticks
- toothpicks
- popsicle sticks
- can openers
- letter openers
- scissors
- knitting needles
- crochet hooks
- screwdrivers
- ice picks
- burnishers
- belt buckles
- paper clips
- hair pins
- fingernails

The emulsion of the SX-70 print remains soft and workable for as long as five days after the picture is ejected from the camera. At first, the emulsion is quite soft; as time progresses, it stiffens until it is impossible to move around. Different results are possible at various stages of the hardening process, and I work on prints throughout the five-day period.

During the first day after ejection, when the emulsion is almost in a liquid state, there is the greatest possibility for changing the image. Colors and forms are easily blended and large areas of pigment can be removed, altering color and form in the most dramatic way. The images of the New York series (numbers 54–59) were worked on in the first hours after development. During this early period, it is difficult to produce very fine lines.

In most cases, I wait a day or so before starting work on a print. The emulsion has by then become firm enough to cause little distortion of the surrounding image, yet is still soft enough to be pulled from one area to another. After four or five days, when the emulsion is almost completely set, I work on fine detail, as in the plate with the ear of corn (number 5) or the kimono (numbers 60–61). I also do most of the dotting at this time. Dots made during the last days are sharply defined whereas dots made earlier have a more diffused look. If the emulsion is too soft, each new dot tends to cancel the previous one.

For practical purposes, there are two distinct emulsion layers in a developed print: the visible color layer that comprises the photographic image and a layer of white pigmented reagent underneath the image. When any pressure is applied to the print, the top color image layer mixes with the white pigment underneath, resulting in the white or gray areas obvious in almost all the pictures in this book. The black lines in many of the pictures are not part of the emulsion but rather the result of having pressed hard

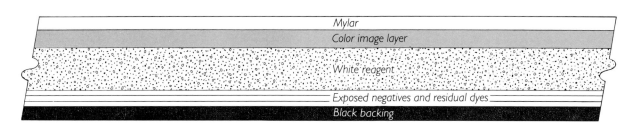

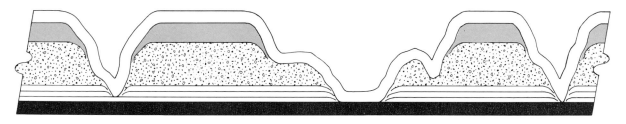

CROSS-SECTION OF SX-70 PRINT AFTER DEVELOPMENT (TOP); AFTER HAND WORKING (BOTTOM)

enough to break through the emulsion entirely, exposing the black backing of the print.

Applying pressure makes an indentation in the print, giving each picture a three-dimensional quality that is not apparent in the reproductions in this book. The actual finished prints look much like ceramic tiles. If large areas of emulsion are removed, the mylar separates from the black backing, creating a silvery,

layered effect. I consider these dimensional qualities further variables in the final print.

Because I tend to wait for the emulsion to firm up a bit before starting to work, I apply a good deal of pressure. The amount of pressure needed depends not only on the stiffness of the emulsion but also on the surface on which the drawing is made and the type of tool used. Hard surfaces such as formica or marble require the least pressure. Wooden tables or cutting boards require more, and sometimes make it difficult to draw smooth lines. They are good, however, for adding textural qualities in large areas that are heavily worked. Metal tools seem more responsive than wooden ones.

The mylar surface of the SX-70 print is very tough, and I have never cut or broken through it accidentally, although sharp tools can scratch the mylar.

The physical characteristics of the emulsion can be altered somewhat by heating or cooling the SX-70 prints. Heating will soften the emulsion and make it more workable. This softening is temporary; after cooling, the print returns to its former state and in fact hardens faster than normal. A print that is completely hardened, however, cannot be made workable by heating.

Freezing an SX-70 print after the image is fully developed can retard the hardening process indefinitely. If I shoot more film than I expect to work on within five days, I will freeze some of the prints and save them until later. Once thawed, the prints reassume their normal properties and can be drawn on as usual.

FROZEN PRINT

If a print is put into a freezer immediately after it is ejected from the camera, the normal development process will be permanently retarded. The resulting photograph will exhibit delicate, pastel colors. The picture of the two pale roses and the out-of-focus figure (above) illustrates this technique. This print was placed in the kitchen freezer immediately after being ejected, taken out several days later, and then slightly altered by hand work.

TOASTED PRINT

PRINT MADE WITH INCANDESCENT LIGHT

When I first began experimenting with SX-70 prints, some visiting friends dropped a print into an electric toaster. The print bubbled, cracked, and became generally distorted. Since then, I have occasionally toasted some of my prints, such as the picture of the mirror (above). I drew on that print both before and after toasting. Toasting prints is very unpredictable and I am often not satisfied with the resulting prints as finished pieces. When my work begins to get tight or repetitive, however, I'll toast a print, simply for the surprise.

I use a flashbar for a great many of my photographs. The flash illuminates evenly, provides maximum sharpness and definition, and produces highly saturated and well-balanced color. It also creates a shadow around the subject which guides me in drawing. In addition, the flash tends to flatten perspective and volume, a quality which I take further with the drawing technique.

Recently I have begun to take more photographs without flash. With less light, as in indoor situations, the camera uses slower shutter speeds and wider apertures, reducing sharpness and diffusing the colors. Shooting without flash allows the film to capture color qualities which result from varying temperatures of the light source and from incidental reflected light. Our eyes adjust automatically to these variations and we tend not to perceive them, but color film is very sensitive to these shifts.

The picture of the tulips (previous page) was taken at night in a room lit by incandescent light bulbs. The photographs numbered 42–43 (Blue Suzy) were taken in a cool room in early morning. The room was lit through a window to the left of the figure, and outside the window was a dark, blue-green garden reflecting its light and influence into the room. The Calistoga bottles (numbers 34–35) were photographed in the corner of a room with lavender walls. The picture was made in mid-afternoon on a warm, sunny day. Through experimentation, one can predict the colors that will predominate in different lighting situations. I enjoy seeing the subjects presented in these new ways.

SEQUENCE OF HAND WORKED IMAGES

To better illustrate the various changes that take place during the drawing process, I have included three virtually identical images (above) that have been hand worked to different stages of completion. The first of the three images has been left unaltered; the second has been worked to an intermediate stage; the third has been completed. This sequence shows how my work might progress on a single print.

It is difficult to start drawing on a good picture. The first lines inevitably detract from the impact of the original; they appear rough, crude, and awkward compared to the soft colors and clarity of the un- altered print. In the first of the illustrations, there is a luminosity in the bottle and a beautiful quality of light around the leaves in the upper right portion of the picture. Once the drawing starts, the seeming per- fection of the original is violated.

In most cases my first step is to outline the principle forms of the picture. I do this rather cautiously. Dur- ing this process I try not to distort the appearance of the objects themselves. When this initial outlining is completed, as seen in the second illustration, the photograph is at its weakest; it has lost the subtlety of the unworked image but has not gained the strength of a finished piece. The second illustration identifies the elements of the picture but does not declare their importance. It seems that every photograph I hand work must become worse before becoming better. Beyond this point is where I learn the most and risk the most.

After outlining the objects in the illustration piece, I began strengthening the presence of the figure and the newspaper. I wanted them to be clearer and to be read simultaneously with the bottle. In the unworked photograph the figure was hardly apparent except for a bit of shoulder and a hand. In the final illustration the bottle and the plant have become less obvious and the figure and the newspaper have jumped forward. Both the unworked and the fully worked images are interesting, yet the worked image is more direct in its impact and has an abstract quality to which I respond.

The illustration was worked with the dental tool entirely. The fine lines were made with the tip of the tool and the lines in the foreground were made using the broad center section of the tool's curved portion. The white section in the top of the picture was made by crosshatching the shadow areas until all the dark pigment which comprised the shadow was mixed with the layer of white pigment that rested underneath it.

It is not always easy for me to judge when an image is completed. I can usually predict the image as far as the intermediate stage. After that, the print may take very little work to reach completion, quite a bit more, or it might even be worked to death. I generally push myself to work the print as far as possible. I have overworked many of my pictures, but I want to find the point at which the print is at its most powerful and most suggestive.

I consider the drawing process much the same as I do the darkroom process for printing a negative. The hand work clarifies the formal aspects of each piece and at the same time invests it with my personality. I draw on my SX-70 pictures to initiate change and I am constantly looking for surprises.

My photographs have become more abstract over the past year, yet I want them to retain the familiarity of snapshots. My pictures do not necessarily represent the people, places, or events photographed. A photograph borrows something from the event and something from the mind of the photographer. When the picture is finished it has a life of its own.

All of the techniques I have described have been learned through trial and error. I believe it is nearly impossible to adopt someone else's technique. Technique is something that is developed through practice, and is highly individual. At the same time, I have always enjoyed knowing how others work. It is for this reason that I have included this essay.

The photographs themselves need no explanation, but I want to share what I have learned in the hope that the reader will have a better understanding of how this work came about. Should my descriptions encourage others to explore drawing on their own SX-70 images, their experience will likely go beyond any explanation I might offer. Nothing can compare to the fullness of a process unbroken.

Edited by Andrew Fluegelman

Designed by Howard Jacobsen

Text edited by Molly Prescott

Illustrations and production by David Bunnett

Text set in Gill Sans Light by
Michael Sykes and Katherine Parker
Community Type and Design, San Rafael, California

Color separations produced with a
Hell DC-300 laser electronic scanner by
Acme Printing Company, Medford, Massachusetts

Printed and bound using
80-pound Mead Black and White Dull by
Kingsport Press, Kingsport, Tennessee

Norman Locks received a Bachelor of Fine Arts
Degree from the San Francisco Art Institute and a
Master of Arts in Photography from California
State University, San Francisco. He has worked with
the Ansel Adams Gallery in Yosemite National Park
and with the Friends of Photography, Carmel,
California, directing their photography workshop
programs. Mr. Locks currently teaches at the
University of California, Santa Cruz.